The Father's Easter Story

Matthew 27:45–61; Luke 2:52; 3:21–22; 7:22; 22:41–42, 54; 24:50–51; John 3:16–17; 19:1, 15–18; 20:1–23; and Galatians 4:4–5 for Children

Written by Jonathan Schkade
Illustrated by Chris Wold Dyrud

CONCORDIA PUBLISHING HOUSE · SAINT LOUIS

In the fullness of time,
When the world was dark,
I sent down My Son
To be hope's living spark.

From a Bethlehem baby
To a Nazareth youth,
I watched as He grew
In both wisdom and truth.

With joy I declared Him
"My Son, whom I love"
And sent down My Spirit
To appear as a dove.

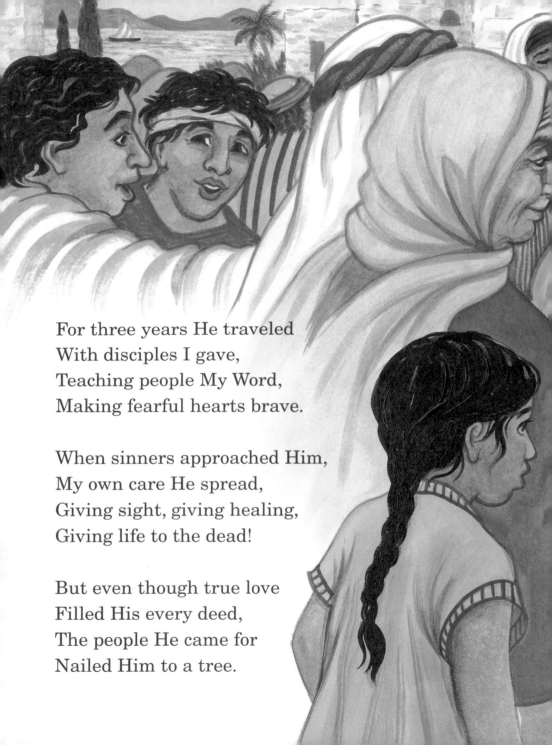

For three years He traveled
With disciples I gave,
Teaching people My Word,
Making fearful hearts brave.

When sinners approached Him,
My own care He spread,
Giving sight, giving healing,
Giving life to the dead!

But even though true love
Filled His every deed,
The people He came for
Nailed Him to a tree.

In the garden He'd asked Me
For some other way.
But there was just one path,
So men took Him that day.

I watched as their whips
Tore His flesh with a crack.
I watched as the soldiers
Put the cross on His back.

They pounded the nails in.
They lifted His cross.
My own perfect Son—
His life for the lost.

And though Jesus pled with
A heart-wrenching yell,
I, God, turned away,
As My Son suffered hell.

Then He died. Jesus died.
His friends all saw doom
As His body was taken
And placed in a tomb.

How I wanted to tell them
Those next three long days
That the end had not happened,
That My Son I would raise.

At last the bright morning
Of Easter arrived,
And My dear Son, Jesus,
Left His tomb alive!

In each amazed face—
Mary, Peter, and all—
I took such delight
When My Son they saw!

Though Jesus ascended
To be by My side,
His friends told His story
To all, far and wide.

My Jesus, you see,
Died wholly for you.
His love, My own love,
Is faithful and true.

There's nothing at all
That I wouldn't give,
To forgive your sins
And allow you to live.

Since He rose from death,
You, too, will revive!
And that's why on Easter
My Son came alive.

Dear Parent:

We generally think of Easter as Jesus' story. And it is! The resurrection is the consummation of His victory over sin, death, and the devil so we might be restored to God. We celebrate with praise and thanksgiving that this victory is ours too: "Just as Christ was raised from the dead by the glory of the Father, we too might walk in newness of life" (Romans 6:4).

Easter is also the Holy Spirit's story because none of it is anything more than a "story" without the faith that all of it is true: "The natural person does not accept the things of the Spirit of God, for they are folly to him, and he is not able to understand them" (1 Corinthians 2:14).

In this book, we read that Easter is God the Father's story because it is the fulfillment of His promise of salvation: "But God shows His love for us in that while we were still sinners, Christ died for us" (Romans 5:8).

As you read this book with your child, you can remind him that the Bible is filled with wonderful stories: Creation. The flood. Miracles and parables. Christmas. Easter. All of them point to one message: the Lord God fulfilled His promise to send us a Savior from sin and give us the hope of eternal life.

This is the story of a heavenly Father who loves us dearly.

The Editor